Toulon Sunshine
A Kid's Guide To Toulon, France

Photography by John D. Weigand
Poetry by Penelope Dyan

Bellissima Publishing, LLC
Jamul, California
www.bellissimapublishing.com

Copyright © 2017 by Penny D. Weigand and John D. Weigand

All rights reserved. No part of this book may be reproduced or transmitted in any form or by any means, electronic or mechanical, including photocopying, recording, or by any other means, or by any information or storage retrieval system, without permission from the publisher.

ISBN 978-1-61477-281-1
First Edition

"Keep your face always toward the sunshine - and shadows will fall behind you."

Walt Whitman

Toulon Sunshine
Bellissima Publishing, LLC

Introduction

Toulon, France has a large military harbor and is home to a major French naval base. In 1486 Provence became part of France. Soon after, in the year 1494, Charles VIII of France, intending to make France a major Meditrranean sea power, and to support his military campaign in Italy, began construction of a military port at Toulon. The Italian campaign failed, and in 1497 the rulers of Genoa, who controlled commerce on that part of the Mediterranean, blockaded the new port. There were many battles after that, that included Toulon. During World War II, after the Allied landings in North Africa, the German Army occupied southern France. This led to scuttling of the French Fleet at Toulon on November 27, 1942. The city was bombed by the Allies in November the following year, and a lot of the port was destroyed. Toulon was liberated by the Free French Forces of General Jean de Lattre de Tassigny on August 28, 1944 in the Battle of Toulon.

Toulon is now a beautiful, peaceful place that you can see as you turn the pages of this 'learn to read book by the award winning author, Penelope Dyan, and photographer, John D. Weigand. To see even more of Toulon, watch the free music video that goes with this book on Bellissimavideo's YouTube channel.

Toulon Sunshine
A Kid's Guide To Toulon, France

Photography by John D. Weigand
Poetry by Penelope Dyan

You arrive at Toulon,
a peaceful harbor
that throughout French history
was fraught with war,
liberated from the Germans by
the Free French Forces
of General Jn de Lattre de Tassigny,
on August 28, 1944!

You see a lovely French home;
and it seems to YOU,
that it sits beneath an afternoon sky,
of an INCREDIBLE shade of blue!

Coming toward you is a bus of red,
and that sunshine blue sky,
remains over YOUR head!

There are clouds above you in the sky.
You watch as FOUR cars go driving by.
You count them aloud,
"One, two, three. four!"
And THEN from around the bend
there comes one MORE!

You see a cafe, a place to eat,
where at tables outside,
YOU can take a seat.
You probably won't find hot dogs sold there,
because the food is more than likely
a FANCY French faire!

As you go up hill
you see a sandwich shop,
and you, Mom and Dad decide to stop!
You EACH choose a sandwich,
and a French pastry so sweet,
that you decide to take back
to your hotel to eat!

You see a submarine ahead,
painted yellow and bright orange-red.
To you it is a mystery.
Dad says,
"It's a part of France's history!"

You stop and look out
over the Mediterranean sea,
which is as blue as blue as it can be!

There is a yellow house
with a red roof and shutters green.
The oh so blue sky. . . AGAIN is seen!
And the sun shines overhead,
right down upon those roofs of red!

And even MORE color lies ahead of you,
buildings of yellow,
with shades of orange, brown
and green,
and (of course) gray AND blue!

And there is a Maritime Museum.
where YOU can go inside,
and you can learn
ALL about the seas and the tide!
Oh, how fun that is to see AND to do!
It is a PERFECT place
for a kid like YOU!

Finally, YOU are back to where
you FIRST began,
staring out at so many boats
as you stand there on the land.
You hear the chimes
of a faraway church clock,
as you stand there, upon THAT dock.
Mom says,
"It's time to go back to the hotel
and to eat."
And so you go back to your room.
for those sandwiches,
and those French pastries so sweet!
And then, as you walk along,
you hear music, an OLD French song!

"If music be the food of love,
play on."

William Shakespeare

Milton Keynes UK
Ingram Content Group UK Ltd.
UKHW050320161023
430636UK00006B/21